Steck-Vaughn
Comprehension Skills

Main Idea 2

by Donna Townsend
   Linda Ward Beech
   Tara McCarthy

STECK-VAUGHN COMPANY
AUSTIN, TEXAS
A Division of National Education Corporation

Project Design and Supervision: The Quarasan Group, Inc.
Northfield, Illinois, U.S.A.

Cover and Title Page Photograph: COMSTOCK INC./Tom Grill

The main idea is the point a writer or speaker is trying to make about a subject. Learning about main ideas helps you decide what is important. For instance, what's the main idea of a football game?

What is a main idea like? Pretend you are in a city. Tall buildings touch the clouds. A wall of people moves down the sidewalk. You may admire one very tall building or recognize a friend, but these smaller parts themselves are not the city. All the small parts together make a whole city. The city is like the main idea, and the people and buildings are details that add to busy city life.

What is a main idea?

The *main idea sentence* of a paragraph tells what the whole paragraph is about. All the other sentences are *details* or small parts that add to the main idea. Often the main idea sentence is the first or last sentence in a paragraph. But you may find a main idea sentence in the middle of a paragraph, too.

This example may help you think of main ideas:

$$8 + 9 + 7 = 24$$
$$\text{detail} + \text{detail} + \text{detail} = \text{main idea}$$

The *8* and *9* and *7* are all like details. They are smaller than their sum, *24*. The *24*, like the main idea, is a bigger number. It is made of many smaller parts.

Try It!

Read this story and underline the main idea sentence.

Ostriches will eat anything. Although the birds usually eat grass, they also eat wood, stones, bones, and gold. In South Africa, the birds are hunted for the diamonds they may swallow. Ostriches kept in zoos have been known to eat wallets, watches, keys, and coins.

The main idea sentence is the first sentence in the story about ostriches. All the other sentences are details. They give examples of what the main idea sentence states.

The main idea could come at the end of a paragraph:

Although ostriches usually eat grass, they also eat wood, stones, bones, and gold. In South Africa the birds are hunted for the diamonds they may swallow. Ostriches kept in zoos have been known to eat wallets, watches, keys, and coins. Ostriches will eat anything.

This book asks you to find main ideas in paragraphs or stories. For instance, read the story and the question below:

> The people of ancient Egypt created an advanced civilization. Over six thousand years ago they developed a calendar with 360 days and 12 months. They could make paper and write. They built huge monuments with machines they had invented.

 The story mainly tells:
  a. how people made paper
  b. what the people of ancient Egypt did
  c. where an ancient calendar was invented
  d. how the people built monuments

The correct answer is *b*. The first sentence of the story says, "The people of ancient Egypt created an advanced civilization." This is the main idea sentence. It is what the people of ancient Egypt did. The other sentences about the calendar, paper-making, writing, and building are all details. They help convince you that the Egyptians had an advanced society.

Sometimes a story does not have a main idea sentence. Then the story is just made of details. You can figure out the main idea after you read all the details in the paragraph. Read the following story. It does not have a main idea sentence. Try to put the details together and come up with a main idea. Then choose a main idea from the list and write the letter of your answer in the blank.

> Microchips provide the power for wristwatches. They are the brains in our computers, and they control robots. These chips are used in video games and space shuttles. They make our cameras, radios, and televisions small and light.

_____ The story mainly tells:
  a. how computers work
  b. why televisions are small
  c. how microchips are used
  d. how cameras are made

Main idea and you

The main idea is often someone's opinion, not a fact. A writer uses details to convince a reader that the opinion is the right one.

Read the main ideas on this page. Each main idea is an opinion. Write some detail sentences to tell why the main idea is true. (The first one is done for you.)

Main Idea: Love is more important than money.
Detail: *Money cannot buy happiness, but love can make you happy.*
Detail: *Love, not money, brings us friends.*
Detail: *Rich people have money, but everyone has love.*

Main Idea: My best friend and I are very much alike.
Detail: _____
Detail: _____
Detail: _____

Main Idea: My favorite food is _____.
Detail: _____
Detail: _____
Detail: _____

Main Idea: The best movie I've ever seen was _____.
Detail: _____
Detail: _____
Detail: _____

Main Idea: Red is the color of anger.
Detail: _____
Detail: _____
Detail: _____

How to use this book

This book has 25 units with 5 stories in each unit. In units 1 through 12 you will read stories that have main idea sentences. In units 13 through 25 you will read stories that do not have main idea sentences. In all the units, read the story, then answer the question by writing the letter of the correct answer in the blank.

When you finish reading and answering the questions, check your answers by looking at pages 60 through 62. Tear out the answer pages and fold them to the unit you are checking. Write the number of correct answers in the *score* box at the top of the unit page. After you finish all of the stories, try "Main Idea: Just for Fun" on pages 56 through 59.

Hints for Better Reading

■ Units 1 through 12: Read the whole story, then ask: which sentence is a sum of all the other sentences? Which sentence is like the whole city? That is the main idea.

■ Units 13 through 25: Read the story, then decide what all of the details have in common. What is the writer trying to tell you?

Challenge Yourself

Are you a good reader? Try this special challenge. Read each story and then answer the questions about it. Then if the story has a main idea sentence in it, write a sentence that uses other words to state the main idea. If the story does not have a main idea sentence, write one.

1.   Imagine testing glass by throwing chickens at it! Sometimes fast-moving airplanes fly through flocks of birds. If the birds hit a plane's windshield, the glass could shatter and cause a crash. Airplane manufacturers have made a chicken cannon that fires rubber chickens at glass windshields. If the windshield doesn't break when the rubber chicken hits it, the designers know the glass can stand the force of a real crash.

2.   The harmless hognose snake is a champion bluffer. When this snake is threatened, it hisses and acts as if it will bite. If you don't run away, the hognose snake "plays dead". It rolls over on its back, wiggling around as if it's in distress. Then it "dies" with its mouth open and tongue hanging out. If you turn it on its stomach, the snake will roll over on its back again.

3.   Doctors think that wearing red-tinted glasses can relieve sadness. Some people get very moody and sad in the winter. These people may be affected by the brief days. Bright lights help some people, but not everyone. The reddish light coming through rose-colored glasses seems to make people feel better.

4.   The Marines had a problem in World War II. Orders were sent in code. But the enemy kept learning the code. Nothing could be kept secret. Then someone thought that Navajo soldiers could help the Marines. Since very few other people could speak Navajo, this language was used as a code. No one on the enemy side knew Navajo either, so the messages stayed secret.

5.   Dogs have been called our best friends, but they are also good helpers. Some dogs are hunting dogs, while others guard animals and property. Boxers and German shepherds are trained to lead blind people. Doctors test some medicines on dogs. A dog named Laika was the first animal in space.

____ **1.** The story mainly tells:
    a. why birds can be dangerous to airplanes
    b. how a chicken cannon tests glass
    c. how big a bird has to be to damage an airplane
    d. how the chicken cannon works

____ **2.** The story mainly tells:
    a. how the hognose snake rolls over
    b. what things frighten the hognose snake
    c. why it is a champion
    d. how the hognose snake protects itself

____ **3.** The story mainly tells:
    a. why happy people wear rose-colored glasses
    b. when some people get sad
    c. how short the daylight is in winter
    d. how colored glasses may help people feel happy

____ **4.** The story mainly tells:
    a. how Navajo people kept secrets
    b. when the secret code was used
    c. how the Marines found a solution
    d. why the original code had to be changed

____ **5.** The story mainly tells:
    a. how many types of dogs there are
    b. what the name of the space dog was
    c. what kind of dogs can lead blind people
    d. how dogs are useful

Unit 2

1. Virgil, a poet in ancient Rome, gave his dead pet a fine funeral. He built a fancy tomb, wrote several poems, and asked friends to mourn with him. It cost about $100,000 to bury—a housefly! Why did he do this? The government was taking rich people's land away. But land with tombs couldn't be taken from the owners. Virgil used the fly's grave to keep his property.

2. Puffed cereal is made in an odd way. The grain (usually rice or wheat) is put in large cannons that are then plugged at one end. The cannons are pushed into an oven and heated to 550 degrees. After 40 minutes, the cannons' plugs are pulled. Hot air rushes into the cannons. Moisture in the cereal grains turns to steam. The grains puff up like popcorn.

3. If you play tennis, you may get *tennis elbow*. But if you like to play video games, then you'll probably get *arcade elbow*. Or you might get *video wrist*. Doctors have been warning kids about the health dangers of playing video games. Besides sore wrists and elbows, video game players can get eyestrain and aching feet. Worst of all is a terrible sickness. It is called *totally broke*.

4. People have long wondered what causes disease. Years ago, people felt illness was due to demons. Others thought sick people had too much blood. Some felt that disease was a punishment from angry gods. People laughed at the idea that germs caused diseases.

5. Most tigers don't eat people. Usually they kill people when they are frightened. But some tigers develop a taste for people. The worst man-eating tiger ate over four hundred people before she was killed. Now in India people are using wired dummies to train tigers not to attack people. When the tigers bite the real-looking dummies, the beasts get a big shock and run away.

_____ **1.** The story mainly tells:
  a. what kind of pet the poet Virgil had
  b. why an odd funeral was held
  c. how the government took land
  d. how much the pet's funeral cost

_____ **2.** The story mainly tells:
  a. what grains are used to make puffed cereals
  b. how cereal is puffed
  c. how hot the ovens are
  d. how the grain is removed from the cannons

_____ **3.** The story mainly tells:
  a. how playing video games can be bad for your health
  b. what video games are best to play
  c. why kids get eyestrain
  d. how people can get _tennis elbow_

_____ **4.** The story mainly tells:
  a. why people thought germs couldn't cause illness
  b. when some people thought demons caused diseases
  c. what people thought caused diseases
  d. why disease was a punishment from the gods

_____ **5.** The story mainly tells:
  a. how to prevent tigers from attacking people
  b. how many people the hungriest tiger in history ate
  c. what tigers like to eat
  d. how tigers are getting a shock

Unit 3

1. Astronauts can faint in space when a sudden change in speed causes blood to collect in their legs. They faint because there is no blood left to carry oxygen to their brains. To prevent fainting, the crew wears a special anti-gravity suit. The trousers are filled with air which forces blood out of the legs and back up to the brain.

2. People who are blind read using a dot code developed by Louis Braille. But books written in braille cost a lot to make. So new machines for people with vision problems use regular books. One device changes the words on a page into words people can feel with their fingers. Another machine actually reads printed words aloud. Computers can be made to read back whatever is typed into them.

3. Most plants get their food from the soil. However, some plants eat insects to get the nitrogen they need as food. Many of these plants smell like rotting meat, so insects are attracted to them. One plant has sticky hairs to catch insects. The leaves of another type of plant trap water to drown insects.

4. Quacks, or fake doctors, say they cure diseases. One said her machine cured cancer. The sick person stood on a metal plate and held wires against the stomach. Of course, it didn't cure anything. People died without treatment by real doctors. The greedy quack didn't care. She got lots of money from desperate people.

5. Government planners accidentally wiped out a deer herd. The deer lived in a park near the Grand Canyon. Mountain lions killed the old, sick, and weak deer. But the officials allowed hunters to kill the lions. The deer herds grew bigger and ate all the grass. Then, many deer starved or died of disease. The balance of nature was ruined because of a human mistake.

_____ **1.** The story mainly tells:
  a. why fainting can be dangerous
  b. who is likely to faint
  c. how fainting among astronauts can be prevented
  d. what happens when the brain lacks blood

_____ **2.** The story mainly tells:
  a. who developed the braille alphabet
  b. who uses the braille code of dots
  c. how machines help people who are blind
  d. how computers read printed words

_____ **3.** The story mainly tells:
  a. where most plants get their food
  b. why plants sometimes have sticky hairs
  c. how some plants catch insects for food
  d. why insects are attracted to certain plants

_____ **4.** The story mainly tells:
  a. whether a quack is a real doctor or not
  b. how the machine was supposed to cure cancer
  c. how a quack fooled sick people
  d. what kind of person will get help from a quack

_____ **5.** The story mainly tells:
  a. what kind of animal hunted the deer
  b. how deer grow bigger
  c. how government planners made a mistake
  d. what killed the deer in the herds

11

Unit 4

1. Many superstitions seem silly. But a superstition from World War I may be based on truth. This is the belief that lighting three cigarettes from one match is unlucky. At night a match that stayed lit long enough to light three cigarettes could be very unlucky. It could draw the enemy's fire.

2. An odd burst of energy in space puzzled astronomer Jocelyn Bell. Friends joked about "little green men" sending messages. So the burst was named *LGM-1*. More signals appeared. Scientists finally found out that stars were exploding and giving off energy. This burst of power that Bell found was called a pulsar.

3. You've heard of Paul Revere's ride. But Sybil Ludington, age 16, made a longer, more courageous ride. In 1777 a rider warned that the British were attacking. Sybil jumped on her horse and went to spread the alarm. She rode 40 miles in one night. The American soldiers she alerted drove the British back to their ships.

4. A professor examined murder reports in Miami for fifteen years. The rate of killings did not stay constant. A chart that noted the dates of the murders and the moon's cycles was made. The professor found that the murder rate was highest when the moon was full.

5. The Siamese fighting fish has interesting habits. An angry male fighting fish changes colors. Its scales turn red, green, blue, and purple. The male Siamese fighting fish also helps hatch the fish eggs. After the eggs are laid, he gathers them into his mouth and blows them into a nest made of bubbles. He then stays on guard to protect the eggs.

_____ **1.** The story mainly tells:
    a. how matches stay lit at night
    b. why superstitions are silly
    c. how soldiers acted during World War I
    d. how one superstition may have begun

_____ **2.** The story mainly tells:
    a. when people thought aliens were sending messages
    b. how pulsars were discovered
    c. why exploding stars give off energy
    d. how little green men send messages

_____ **3.** The story mainly tells:
    a. how far Sybil Ludington rode in one night
    b. who the American soldiers were fighting
    c. what Sybil Ludington did
    d. what happened to Paul Revere on his ride

_____ **4.** The story mainly tells:
    a. how people are murdered in Miami, Florida
    b. what charts are used for
    c. how the moon affects the murder rate
    d. how long the professor worked

_____ **5.** The story mainly tells:
    a. how the male fish helps hatch eggs
    b. how the male fish builds a nest
    c. why the male fish changes colors
    d. what unusual things the fighting fish does

1. If you go to Cocos Island near Costa Rica, take a shovel. Three treasures may be hidden there. The first pirate visiting Cocos hid 100 tons of silver. The second pirate hid 150 tons of gold. The third treasure was buried by a ship captain who had stolen 14 tons of gold and many jewels. But no one has ever found these stolen treasures.

---

2. There is a new science called *ergonomics.* It is the study of how offices can be made more comfortable. Scientists are looking at how furniture, light, colors, and machines affect people. If workers get headaches, their office light could be too bright. If workers get tired too easily, they might need a more cheerful color of paint on their office walls.

---

3. A man in Germany lives in a treehouse. He trained trees to grow toward each other. He tied the branches of some trees together, then fastened nets on the inside and outside for protection. Next, he planted vines to cover the outside. Finally, he laid down foam blocks for the floor and put material on the walls for decoration.

---

4. Centuries ago, people believed in creatures called basilisks. Old myths said these monsters were created when a rooster laid an egg that was hatched by snakes. This reptile was supposed to be able to kill with its breath or a single look. A person with a mirror could kill a basilisk. The sight of the beast's own image scared it to death.

---

5. Doctors are learning how to use imagination to cure disease. People may feel helpless when they are sick. This can make them sicker. Now many patients are taught to pretend their white blood cells are knights fighting diseases. They are also told to think of themselves as completely well. These patients really do get well faster!

_____ **1.** The story mainly tells:
  a. where Cocos Island is located
  b. what you should bring if you go to Cocos Island
  c. what treasures might be hidden on Cocos Island
  d. where the third treasure of Cocos Island came from

_____ **2.** The story mainly tells:
  a. what to do when you get a headache or backache
  b. why it's good to have plants in the office
  c. how offices can be made into better places
  d. why machines in people's offices are harmful

_____ **3.** The story mainly tells:
  a. how a man built a house out of trees
  b. how to train trees to grow toward each other
  c. which materials are for decorating walls
  d. which trees make good houses

_____ **4.** The story mainly tells:
  a. whether the basilisk was a real animal
  b. how people could hunt the deadly basilisk
  c. what people once believed about basilisks
  d. how basilisks were hatched

_____ **5.** The story mainly tells:
  a. how helpless people feel when they're sick
  b. how doctors use white blood cells
  c. how knights fight disease
  d. how imagination can make patients better

1.   Many African people bitten by sick mosquitoes caught malaria, a serious disease. Some people who were bitten stayed well because cells in their bodies changed. These changes in their cells protected them from the illness. Over the years, the helpful change was passed down to their children.

2.   Many books printed in the past 100 years are falling apart. A chemical in the paper causes the paper to crack. Wrapping old books tightly in plastic and freezing them can preserve them. Most librarires are using special gases to stop the paper from cracking.

3.   A black woman who couldn't walk from age 4 to age 6 became "the fastest woman alive." Two serious illneses left Wilma Rudolph's legs weak. But her family helped her to exercise, and she learned to walk again. At age 16, she first ran in the Olympics. At 20, she won three Olympic gold medals.

4.   Interesting laws are in effect today. Dynamite can't be used in fishing since all the fish in the area would die. And even though deer and bears come right into town, hunting on the streets isn't allowed. Hunters might shoot people by accident. Debt collectors can't wear costumes, so they can't dress like police officers to scare people.

5.   Thomas Dewey was running for president during World War II. He found out that the U.S. knew the Japanese code. He thought the president knew the Japanese would attack Pearl Harbor and had let men die on purpose. If Dewey told what he thought, he'd win the election. But the enemy would change their code. So Dewey kept the secret. Later, records showed that the president hadn't known about the code.

_____ **1.** The story mainly tells:
   a. how a change in body cells protected people
   b. what malaria is and how it's spread
   c. where the change in the genes occurred
   d. who is likely to have the change in genes

_____ **2.** The story mainly tells:
   a. how books can be frozen
   b. how old books can be preserved
   c. what causes the paper to become brittle
   d. how much it costs to preserve a book

_____ **3.** The story mainly tells:
   a. how Wilma Rudolph's family helped her
   b. how old she was when she first ran in the Olympics
   c. how Wilma Rudolph overcame her illness
   d. how many records and medals she won in track

_____ **4.** The story mainly tells:
   a. why hunting animals on streets isn't allowed
   b. how dynamite can be used to catch fish
   c. which odd laws are still around today
   d. how debt collectors must dress

_____ **5.** The story mainly tells:
   a. how the U.S. government knew Japan's plans
   b. why Dewey told the people
   c. how Dewey kept a secret
   d. how the Japanese attacked Pearl Harbor

1. Historians are trying to solve the mystery of Stonehenge. This monument in England is a ring of huge stones. Some of the stones weigh 50 tons and were brought from 300 miles away! Some scientists think Stonehenge was a place of worship many years ago. Others think the stones were used to help people predict changes in the sun and moon.

2. Researchers studied snack foods to see which ones caused cavities. Cake, raisins, and bananas caused the most cavities. Chocolate, potato chips, and peanuts weren't quite as bad. Foods with fat coat the teeth and protect them, but sticky foods cling. The acids in sticky foods have more time to rot the teeth.

3. Lasers are instruments that produce a special kind of light. The light of a laser is very narrow. It doesn't spread out like sunlight does. The beam is powerful because the light is concentrated. Some laser beams cut through steel. Other lasers can be used to send television signals. Doctors use lasers to burn diseased cells, to do eye operations, or to close wounds. Lasers are useful new scientific tools.

4. Pearls are formed when an oyster swallows a bit of sand. The oyster covers the sand grain with nacre. This smooth, shiny substance keeps the sand from hurting the oyster and grows into a pearl. As the pearl grows, it can become white, black, pink, orange, purple, or golden. From tiny bits of sand, the oyster can grow a pearl that weighs over fourteen pounds and costs over thirty-two million dollars!

5. A Greek myth tells how a man named Daedalus created wings and flew. Now scientists are building the *Daedalus project*. They are making an airplane that can be pedaled like a bicycle. The light plane will have a 50-foot wingspan. This type of plane might someday allow astronauts to fly on Mars.

_____ **1.** The story mainly tells:
   a. where the Stonehenge monument is located
   b. how big the rocks at Stonehenge are
   c. how far some of the Stonehenge rocks were carried
   d. what scientists think Stonehenge was

_____ **2.** The story mainly tells:
   a. why cake causes tooth decay
   b. when sweet foods cause cavities in teeth
   c. what foods affect the number of cavities
   d. why fatty foods are very likely to cause cavities

_____ **3.** The story mainly tells:
   a. whether a laser beam is wide or narrow
   b. why a laser's light is so powerful
   c. how laser beams help people
   d. what things can be cut with a laser

_____ **4.** The story mainly tells:
   a. how pearls are formed
   b. what colors natural pearls may be
   c. what sea animals can create pearls
   d. what the biggest pearl in the world is worth

_____ **5.** The story mainly tells:
   a. who Daedalus was and what he did
   b. what the *Daedalus project* is
   c. how long the *Daedalus project* flight will be
   d. how the special plane will be powered

19

Unit 8

1. Dolls are popular toys today, but they had other uses in the past. The Hopis used sacred dolls to teach children about spirits. In ancient Egypt, dolls were sometimes buried with people. These dolls would be servants in the ghost world. Dolls dressed in fancy clothes showed pioneer women in America how the styles had changed.

2. Strange winds may make some people in Europe and North Africa feel bad. These winds are called *Siroccos,* and they are found near mountains or deserts. Some people get headaches or can't sleep when the winds blow. Other people have accidents or get angry. A chemical in people's bodies increases when the winds blow. Scientists think this may explain why some people feel sick.

3. A new medicine for wounds has been found—sugar! Some patients were sick with skin ulcers. These are ugly open sores that don't heal. A doctor tried sugar and found that it worked. Since then, sugar has been used on over three thousand injuries. French doctors tried the treatment on people who had heart operations and found the sugared wounds healed much faster than usual.

4. People used to dance to cure spider bites. Taranto, an Italian town, had a lot of spiders called tarantulas. People feared these ugly, harmless spiders. They thought that a bite could kill. Fast dancing was supposed to make people sweat and lose the spider's poison. A country dance called the tarantella got its start because of this belief.

5. Scientists have tried teaching chimpanzees how to talk. But chimps can't speak with words. So they are learning the sign language used by people who are deaf. The chimps ask questions and create new words, such as *red drink fruit* for *watermelon.* Some even try to teach sign language to other animals.

_____ 1. The story mainly tells:
   a. why dolls were sometimes buried
   b. what purposes dolls have served
   c. which Indian tribe used sacred dolls
   d. how people learned about fashion from dolls

_____ 2. The story mainly tells:
   a. why some people get sick
   b. how certain winds may affect people's health
   c. why winds blow near mountains
   d. where the strange winds are likely to occur

_____ 3. The story mainly tells:
   a. who first thought of using sugar on wounds
   b. how sugar can help heal wounds
   c. how many people have been treated with sugar
   d. how sugar has been used in heart operations

_____ 4. The story mainly tells:
   a. what town in Italy had a lot of spiders
   b. whether the Italian tarantulas were poisonous
   c. how a dance got its name
   d. how country dances were created

_____ 5. The story mainly tells:
   a. what kind of monkeys are learning to talk
   b. what language the chimps use in the tests
   c. how chimps are learning language
   d. whether other animals can learn special languages

Unit 9

1. Imagine cheating in a World Series! In 1919, someone paid eight Chicago White Sox baseball players to lose games in the series. The people who paid the players bet money that the men would lose the games. The betters hoped to make a lot of money. The players who cheated were severely punished. They were never allowed to play baseball again.

2. The peanut is the humble plant with hundreds of functions. Most peanuts are roasted in the shell and lightly salted. About half the peanuts eaten in the U.S. are ground into a thick paste called *peanut butter.* The rich oil made from peanuts is good for frying foods. Peanut oil is also used to oil machines and to make soaps, paint, and explosives. Even the peanut shell is used in plastics and to fertilize the soil.

3. The lack of gravity in space makes even simple tasks a challenge. Astronauts have to wear boots that hold their feet to the floor so they can walk around. Eating is a real chore. Dried and frozen food is stored in plastic bags. To eat chicken soup, the astronauts cut a hole in one end of the bag and squeeze the soup into their mouths.

4. A radio story called "The War of the Worlds" once started a panic. A lot of people didn't hear that it was just a story about monsters from space. They thought the fake news bulletins were true. People were frantic. It took hours to calm them down and convince them it was only a radio play.

5. Some college teachers in Michigan have made a small computer that looks like an apple. It will be picked and handled like real fruit. Much fruit is damaged on its way to market. So this machine will measure shaking and temperature changes. The computerized apple will help people find ways to avoid damaging fruits during shipping.

_____ **1.** The story mainly tells:
    a. which city the baseball players were from
    b. who paid the players
    c. how people cheated during a World Series
    d. how the guilty players were punished

_____ **2.** The story mainly tells:
    a. why peanut oil is used for frying
    b. how much peanut butter is eaten in the U.S.
    c. how many uses the peanut has
    d. why peanut shells make good fertilizer

_____ **3.** The story mainly tells:
    a. why there is little gravity in space
    b. how astronauts adapt to low-gravity conditions
    c. why a lot of space food is in plastic bags
    d. how to eat chicken soup

_____ **4.** The story mainly tells:
    a. what people thought about news stories
    b. why people were afraid of the monsters
    c. how a radio play fooled many people
    d. where the monsters in the story came from

_____ **5.** The story mainly tells:
    a. where the computerized apple was created
    b. how the computer company helped make the machine
    c. what the computerized apple looks like
    d. what the computerized apple is for

23

Unit 10

1.   Many people in India don't eat beef. Even though they don't eat them, people find many uses for cattle in that country. The cows eat garbage and weeds that people cannot eat. Cows give milk, which is a valuable food. Young cattle plow fields and carry big loads.

2.   There are ways to learn about people besides talking to them or watching them. Look at the floor. You can tell where people walk because that's where the carpet is worn. The next time you're in another person's car, listen to the radio. Different people tune in to different stations. You can find out if people are on a diet by looking in their refrigerators.

3.   Diamonds are so hard that they can cut through almost any metal. So they are often used in industrial work. Sometimes whole diamonds are set into tools. Other times, dust from crushed stones is used to coat tool edges. The strange thing is that if diamonds are exposed to extreme heat, they may turn into graphite. That's the same soft material pencil leads are made of!

4.   A scientist found out that millions of animals died every 26 million years. He thinks comets caused the deaths. Comets exploded as they slammed into the earth. The dust from the explosion blocked light and heat from the sun. The animals and plants on the earth couldn't live in the cold.

5.   A jeweler named Fabergé made Easter eggs of rare metals and jewels. They were often given as gifts by a Russian emperor. The elaborate eggs are only a few inches high. Some of the eggs have tiny clocks inside them. Others have small pictures or toys. The highest price ever paid for a Fabergé egg was over one million five hundred thousand dollars!

_____ **1.** The story mainly tells:
   a. how cows are used in India
   b. where some people do not eat beef
   c. which cows plow fields
   d. what milk is used for

_____ **2.** The story mainly tells:
   a. how to tell where people walk
   b. how to learn about people
   c. how to listen to the radio
   d. how to watch people

_____ **3.** The story mainly tells:
   a. how to turn a diamond into graphite
   b. how diamonds are used in industry
   c. how diamond dust coats tool edges
   d. when diamonds are used in pencils

_____ **4.** The story mainly tells:
   a. how often animals died
   b. why comets may come near the earth
   c. where the dust comes from
   d. what may explain animal deaths in the past

_____ **5.** The story mainly tells:
   a. what Fabergé eggs are like
   b. who bought and gave the eggs as gifts
   c. what Fabergé eggs have in them
   d. how Fabergé made the eggs

Unit 11

1. Spices were important in ancient times. They made everyday food taste better. Doctors told people to eat spices to stay healthy. The strong flavors of the spices hid the taste of spoiled food. Rich people showed their wealth by using many spices in cooking.

2. Could you catch a baseball that is going two miles a minute? Gabby Street of the Washington Senators did. A friend wondered if Gabby could catch a baseball dropped from the 555-foot-high Washington Monument. So in 1908 a man dropped 13 balls from the monument. The wind blew almost all of the baseballs out of reach. But Gabby caught the last one as it plunged down.

3. The tulip was very popular in the 1600's. Dutch people bought the bulbs, hoping to make money. One tulip bulb sold for twelve tons of grain, twenty-four animals, and some fancy clothes. But soon no one would pay high prices for the tulip bulbs. Many people who bought tulips lost all their money. Finally the government had to control the trade in bulbs.

4. Each year experts study the movie habits of Americans. The study shows some interesting facts. For example, did you know that teenagers go to more movies than any other age group? Almost half of all Americans are over forty. But only 15 of every 100 movie-goers are in this age group. This explains the big success of movies about teenagers.

5. Scientists thought for a long time that a certain kind of fish had been extinct for 60 million years. But in 1938 a living fish of that type was caught near South Africa. Another fish like the first one was caught near the Comoro Islands. The people of the islands had eaten the fish for years. They used the scales of the fish to patch bicycle tires. While scientists thought the fish was rare, the people thought it was ordinary.

_____ **1.** The story mainly tells:
    a. how food was kept from spoiling
    b. how spices were used long ago
    c. how some people stayed healthy
    d. when people used spices a lot

_____ **2.** The story mainly tells:
    a. where the baseballs were dropped
    b. how Gabby Street caught a fast ball
    c. how fast the baseballs fell
    d. what team Gabby Street played for

_____ **3.** The story mainly tells:
    a. what flower was popular in the 1600's
    b. how much one bulb sold for
    c. where the flower craze took place
    d. how tulip prices led to government controls

_____ **4.** The story mainly tells:
    a. what movie habits Americans have
    b. what movie habits teenagers have
    c. why teenagers like movies
    d. why the smallest group of movie-goers is over 40

_____ **5.** The story mainly tells:
    a. what scientists discovered about a fish
    b. why a certain kind of fish was extinct
    c. how the scales of a fish were used to patch tires
    d. how scientists caught a rare type of fish

1. The earth's surface is made up of about twenty rigid plates or sections of earth. These plates move slowly past each other. As they move, the rocks at the edges of the plates are squeezed and pulled apart. When the force of the movement is too great, the rocks shift and shatter, causing an earthquake.

2. Rescuers fought to free a man caught in a burning truck. The metal was so badly twisted that even a wrecker couldn't budge it. Suddenly, a stranger ripped a door off the cab with his hands. He twisted the steering wheel away and braced his shoulders under the crushed top to lift it. Later, people found out that the stranger once lost a child in a fire. His hatred of fire apparently gave him the strength to save the trapped man.

3. North Carolina police may use germs to catch bank thieves. Important papers can be sprayed with harmless germs. The germs will stick to the hands of anyone who touches the paper. If a dishonest employee steals the papers, things he or she touches later will have the germs on them. A scientist can show that the person who left the germs got them when stealing the treated papers.

4. Annie Oakley was famous for her shooting. She learned to shoot when she was only eight. At fifteen, she won a shooting match against a great marksman. For many years she performed in Buffalo Bill's Wild West Show. Once when she was in England, the Prince of Wales gave Annie a silver cup. Written there was, "You are the best shot I have ever seen."

5. A French company found that people can make food out of oil. Fertilizers are added to the oil. Oxygen is then pumped through the liquid. This mixture encourages the growth of high-protein yeasts. The tasteless, odorless yeasts are used to feed starving people.

_____ 1. The story mainly tells:
   a. what makes up the earth's surface
   b. how the plates form a surface
   c. how earthquakes happen
   d. how plates move

_____ 2. The story mainly tells:
   a. how a man got caught in a fire
   b. how to get someone out of a wrecked truck
   c. how strong the stranger was
   d. how a man's emotions helped him save a life

_____ 3. The story mainly tells:
   a. how some germs are harmless to people
   b. when crooked bank employees steal important things
   c. how police use germs to solve crimes
   d. how important papers are treated

_____ 4. The story mainly tells:
   a. when Buffalo Bill's Wild West Show performed
   b. why Annie Oakley was famous
   c. when the Prince of Wales gave Annie a cup
   d. how Frank Butler met Annie

_____ 5. The story mainly tells:
   a. how food can be made from oil
   b. what fertilizers are added to the mixture
   c. what the food yeasts taste and smell like
   d. which people eat the yeast foods

1.   Imagine buying groceries with piles of money! Germany had a terrible money problem after World War I. Almost everyone had plenty of cash, since the government printed lots of money. But everything cost a lot because the cash was almost worthless. A sack of bills might buy one loaf of bread. One woman left a laundry basket of cash alone for a minute. While she was gone, a thief stole the basket, but left the money!

2.   If you were invited to dinner in the middle ages, you would have to be certain to wash your hands. People back then had only spoons and their fingers to eat with, and they shared plates. Scratching an itch at the table was also impolite. You might carry the flea that was biting you to the common food dish. After dinner you threw the bones on the floor to the dogs.

3.   Albert Einstein was one of the greatest scientists of all time. Yet he failed almost all his classes in high school. Thomas Edison, the inventor, attended school for only three months. Harriet Tubman was a slave with no formal schooling. Yet she used her knowledge of the forest to help over three hundred people escape from slavery!

4.   According to a myth, the gods gave King Midas one wish. The greedy king wished that everything he touched would turn to gold. He enjoyed making his palace gold, but he soon cursed the gift. He tried to eat, but the food itself became gold. Midas asked the gods to remove the golden touch and the gods answered his prayer.

5.   Bamboo is a giant grass. It grows very fast. One type of bamboo grows 3 feet in 24 hours! The bamboo is hollow and light, but very strong. Bamboo is so strong it can be made into fences, roofs, boats, and furniture. However, young bamboo is tender, and people eat the beautiful green shoots.

_____ 1. The story mainly tells:
   a. how bad the money problem was in Germany
   b. what a thief stole
   c. how much money people in Germany had
   d. how the government printed money

_____ 2. The story mainly tells:
   a. what table manners were like in the Middle Ages
   b. where people threw bones after dinner
   c. why scratching at dinner was bad manners
   d. why people ate with spoons

_____ 3. The story mainly tells:
   a. why Albert Einstein failed classes
   b. how people did great things without schooling
   c. why Thomas Edison was taught at home
   d. how Harriet Tubman used her knowledge

_____ 4. The story mainly tells:
   a. why Midas earned a wish
   b. what Midas's wish was
   c. how Midas' wish was really a mistake
   d. how the gods answered Midas' request

_____ 5. The story mainly tells:
   a. how fast bamboo can grow
   b. what the bamboo looks like
   c. how people eat bamboo plants
   d. what the bamboo plant is like

Score

31

1. A clerk made a two-million-dollar mistake because he was careless about a comma. He was supposed to write, "All foreign fruit plants are free from duty." That sentence allowed growers to import fruit trees without paying taxes. Instead, he wrote, "All foreign fruit, plants are free from duty." Adding the comma let people import both fruits and plants without paying taxes. The U.S. lost two million dollars in taxes.

2. "Gold! I see gold!" Howard Carter exclaimed. He was an archeologist and he had just opened King Tut's tomb. Inside, he saw golden chairs, jeweled necklaces, and battle trumpets that had been silent for thousands of years. King Tut's mummy was found inside a solid gold case that was over six feet long!

3. People used to play football bareheaded. After many injuries, players began to use plain leather caps. Plastic helmets and masks appeared later. Still, many players were getting hurt. To make the best helmets, designers studied— woodpeckers! Their tough, spongy skulls became the model for modern football helmets.

4. Mary Ann Bickerdyke organized Union Army hospitals in the Civil War. She fought to get good food and clothing for the sick soldiers. Once she found a doctor wearing a shirt and shoes that were for patients. Mary Ann pushed him down and pulled off the clothes. The soldiers cheered and laughed. The embarrassed doctor asked for a transfer to another hospital.

5. Light-colored trees grew in England. On these trees rested light-colored moths. Since the moths were the same color as the trees, birds could not see the insects to eat them. Then cities grew up. Dirty air turned the trees in the cities a dark color. Birds could see the light-colored moths and eat them. A few of the moths were born a dark color, however. They could hide on the dirty trees, lay their eggs, hatch their young, and survive in the modern world.

_____ **1.** The story mainly tells:
   a. how much money was lost
   b. how an error cost a lot of money
   c. why fruit and plants should be taxed
   d. how people pay taxes when they import items

_____ **2.** The story mainly tells:
   a. what Howard Carter did for a living
   b. what was found in King Tut's tomb
   c. where the king's mummy was found
   d. what the mummy case was made of

_____ **3.** The story mainly tells:
   a. why football helmets must be strong and light
   b. when leather caps were used in football
   c. where designers found a model for a perfect helmet
   d. why many players are injured

_____ **4.** The story mainly tells:
   a. why Mrs. Bickerdyke helped the Union Army
   b. why the doctor was so embarrassed
   c. how Mrs. Bickerdyke embarrassed a doctor
   d. what items the doctor had stolen from patients

_____ **5.** The story mainly tells:
   a. how moths adapted to their surroundings
   b. how birds find moths on trees
   c. what color trees can be in cities
   d. how cities grew

1. In 1692 in Massachusetts, some girls decided they did not like their neighbors. So the girls accused the neighbors of being witches. The girls said they were cut, pinched, and choked by strange visitors who looked like their neighbors. Many people were arrested, and twenty people were put to death. But one man accused of being a wizard said he would file a lawsuit against the girls. The girls took back their lies.

2. Two boys were severely burned. They had almost no healthy skin left. Doctors took a stamp-sized piece of skin from one boy and grew a square yard of it in the laboratory. Doctors put the healthy, new skin on the hurt children and the boys lived. Perhaps this process may help burned patients in the future.

3. British soldiers in a German prison camp decided to tunnel out. They built an exercise bench. For weeks, the British soldiers jumped over it for "exercise." But men hidden inside the bench slowly dug a tunnel over one hundred feet long. Three men escaped through the tunnel to England.

4. If someone stops breathing, lay the victim on his or her back. With your finger, check the mouth to make sure there is nothing the victim can swallow. Then start *mouth-to-mouth resuscitation*. Tilt the person's head back so the chin points upward. Hold the person's nose, take a deep breath, and breathe into the mouth. Finally, turn your head and listen to make sure the air comes back out of the lungs.

5. Seeing Eye dogs work for a living. They are the eyes for people who cannot see. The dogs begin training when they are just a year old. They learn how to guide a person around trees and across busy streets. Next, people who are blind spend a month learning the dog's signals. Then the dogs begin their long and helpful careers.

_____ 1. The story mainly tells:
   a. which people the girls disliked
   b. how some girls caused trouble
   c. who said he would file a lawsuit
   d. where the witchcraft trials were held

_____ 2. The story mainly tells:
   a. how doctors saved two burn victims
   b. how the two boys were injured
   c. how doctors use a laboratory
   d. how much skin was grown in the lab

_____ 3. The story mainly tells:
   a. what the men did for exercise
   b. why the prisoners enjoyed sports
   c. how some prisoners carried out a great escape
   d. how long the tunnel was

_____ 4. The story mainly tells:
   a. how to perform mouth-to-mouth resuscitation
   b. how to save people
   c. how to check the victim's mouth
   d. how to make sure the air comes back out

_____ 5. The story mainly tells:
   a. when dogs begin their training
   b. how people learn the dog's signals
   c. why training guide dogs takes a long time
   d. how dogs become Seeing Eye dogs

1. Potatoes were a big crop in Ireland. People raised grain and cows to sell, but they lived off of their potatoes. Suddenly, in 1845, the potato plants died. Over seven hundred thousand people starved to death. Others moved to the U.S., seeking a better life.

2. A scientist took some baby monkeys from their mothers. Each baby monkey was put in a cage by itself. The scientist gave each one a doll that looked like its mother, but the babies were not allowed to see others of their own kind. When the monkeys were grown, they were put in cages with other monkeys. But they didn't like the other monkeys, and some even rejected their own babies.

3. Corn was first grown by Native Americans. They showed Pilgrims how to grow it for food. At one time corn was used as money by the pioneers. A lot of corn is fed to farm animals. People eat it as a vegetable. Oil, starch, and sugar can be made from corn. Corn is also important in industry. Medicine, paper, fertilizer, and glue can be made from corn and corn products.

4. Atom bombs landed on two Japanese cities during World War II. Many people died in the explosions and fires. Later, people in the bombed cities felt weak and tired. They lost their hair and developed big bruises. Women in the area often gave birth to dead babies. Years later, people were still dying from cancer.

5. The Young Pony Express riders often had to drive their horses through rivers. The weather was usually hot and dry. The riders were often afraid because they had to pass through Native American territory. They usually travelled 75 miles a day. For all this, the riders were paid about one hundred dollars a month.

_____ **1.** The story mainly tells:
    a. when potatoes were an important food for the Irish
    b. what happened when the Irish potato crop failed
    c. how many people starved
    d. when people came to America

_____ **2.** The story mainly tells:
    a. what happened to monkeys raised alone
    b. how monkeys act
    c. what kinds of cages monkeys lived in
    d. how some monkeys ignored their babies

_____ **3.** The story mainly tells:
    a. what kind of animals eat corn
    b. how important corn is
    c. who first grew corn for food
    d. who used corn instead of money

_____ **4.** The story mainly tells:
    a. how bombs caused explosions
    b. when people died from cancer
    c. what effects atom bombs caused
    d. what happened in World War II

_____ **5.** The story mainly tells:
    a. how far Pony Express riders rode in a day
    b. what the life of a Pony Express rider was like
    c. how much money a Pony Express rider made
    d. what the weather was like

1. Liu Shih-kun was a skilled musician. In the early 1960's, the Chinese government disliked his piano music. Because he refused to play what they wanted, he spent over seven years in jail. Although he couldn't play his piano there, he could practice in his mind. When he got out, he played just as well as before.

2. CAT scanners are used by doctors, not vets. *CAT* stands for *computerized axial tomography.* The scanner is an X-ray machine that photographs soft tissue. A special dye is put into a person. The machine then takes hundreds of photos. A high-speed computer combines the photos to show the person's organs. Doctors can examine organs this way. The CAT scanner reduces the need for an operation.

3. Before printing was invented, people wrote each book by hand. They decorated the pages with fabulous pictures. Sometimes people wrote books in silver and gold ink. Only the rich could buy books. In the 1300's a Bible cost enough money to pay an average worker for 26 years.

4. Many babies once died from bad milk. Although disease germs could be killed by heating the milk, the milk companies didn't think this was necessary. Then Nathan Straus, a rich man, sold milk for pennies. But his milk had been carefully heated. When people who drank Straus's milk stayed well, health officials realized that boiling milk was important. Soon all milk sold in cities was heated, and the disease rate dropped.

5. In ancient Rome, emperors tried to make the people happy by giving grain away. This charity was supposed to relieve poverty. But people began insisting free food was a basic right. At one time, nearly one out of three people got free wheat. The Roman government nearly ran out of money giving away grain, meat, and oil.

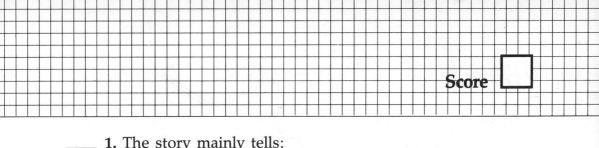

_____ 1. The story mainly tells:
   a. how long Liu Shih-kun stayed in prison
   b. how prison could not change Liu Shih-kun's skills
   c. why the Chinese government didn't like music
   d. what kind of instrument Liu Shih-kun played

_____ 2. The story mainly tells:
   a. who uses a CAT scanner
   b. what *CAT* stands for
   c. how the CAT scanner helps doctors
   d. what kind of computer is used

_____ 3. The story mainly tells:
   a. how much a Bible cost long ago
   b. how printing was invented
   c. how valuable books were long ago
   d. how books were written in gold

_____ 4. The story mainly tells:
   a. how to kill disease germs in milk
   b. how Straus changed the milk business
   c. why companies thought heating milk was unimportant
   d. why Straus was a generous man

_____ 5. The story mainly tells:
   a. how emperors gave food away
   b. when people got free food
   c. how the Roman food program failed
   d. what Roman emperors gave away

1.   Many trees in Greek forests were cut down because the wood was needed for ships. At first the local farmers were happy. They had more cleared land for planting. But rain began washing away the good topsoil. Later, people cut down shallow-rooted trees to make room for valuable olive trees. More erosion occurred, and large sections of Greece became barren.

2.   A store was selling some blue jeans that were stained. People bought the jeans. Some people put the stained jeans on right away. Others washed them first, then put them on. The people who did not wash their jeans got sick. The people who washed them stayed well. Later, doctors found out that the stains on the jeans were a kind of poison.

3.   The Sager family was going to Oregon, but the mother and father died suddenly. John Sager and his six brothers and sisters decided that they would keep traveling. Knowing that adults would object, the kids secretly went away on foot. They walked 500 miles over plains and snow-covered mountains. The weather was bad, and one sister broke a leg. But they kept on until they reached Oregon.

4.   In ancient times, people made the measurements for the great pyramids with string. Two hundred years ago people made chairs with wooden pegs instead of with nails. They also made door hinges out of leather. Today builders still use a string with a weight on the end to make sure bricks are straight.

5.   In 1943, the Nazis planned to capture the Jewish people of Warsaw, Poland. To escape the Nazis, the people smuggled in rifles and built bombs. With these weapons, they faced Nazi soldiers who were armed with tanks and machine guns. After 28 days of war, the Jewish people lost their desperate fight.

_____ 1. The story mainly tells:
    a. what was made with the trees
    b. how cutting down trees caused erosion
    c. why the farmers in Greece were happy at first
    d. what kind of tree was considered valuable

_____ 2. The story mainly tells:
    a. which people got sick
    b. what happened with poisoned jeans
    c. what a store was selling
    d. what doctors think about jeans

_____ 3. The story mainly tells:
    a. how the children made a dangerous trip alone
    b. why adults didn't want the children to go
    c. why John was responsible for the others
    d. how some of the children got sick during the trip

_____ 4. The story mainly tells:
    a. how string is used
    b. how people measured the pyramids
    c. how simple objects are used in construction
    d. how door hinges are made from leather

_____ 5. The story mainly tells:
    a. when rifles and bombs are used for fighting tanks
    b. how long the people fought
    c. how some people refused to go quietly to death
    d. why Nazis wanted to capture the Jewish people

Unit 19

1.   Computers have changed a lot over the years. An early machine added together eighteen million numbers an hour. One person would have needed many years to do the same job. A modern computer recently added 1.5 trillion numbers. It took only three hours!

2.   The beaver's front teeth have a hard, bright orange covering. These teeth are used to cut and tear the bark off trees. The back teeth are flat and rough and are used for chewing. Between the front and back teeth are two flaps of skin. These flaps keep water and splinters from entering the beaver's mouth.

3.   In 1944, a magazine printed a story about a very powerful bomb called the atom bomb. The descriptions in the magazine were quite close to the truth about the bomb. The FBI thought this top-secret information was stolen, but the author had read the details in public records.

4.   Some Puritans hated England, their home. The king would not let them practice their religion as they pleased. They decided to sail to America, which the English had begun to settle. In America, they made some strict laws. Everybody had to be a Puritan or leave. Quakers were whipped in public, and priests were hung. People did not have freedom of religion until 1791.

5.   Product codes on items consist of bars and numbers on the product label. The first numbers tell which company made the item. The last numbers identify the product and size. A laser reads the bars at the checkout. A computer finds the price for that product and prints the price on the cash register slip. Store owners can change prices of items by changing the computer. The records in the computer help the owners learn which goods sell well.

_____ **1.** The story mainly tells:
   a. who uses computers
   b. how long one person takes to do a job
   c. how computers have gotten faster over time
   d. how fast modern computers can add

_____ **2.** The story mainly tells:
   a. what color the front teeth are
   b. what the two flaps of skin are for
   c. how the beaver's mouth is specially made
   d. how splinters get in the beaver's mouth

_____ **3.** The story mainly tells:
   a. how someone worked on a bomb
   b. what FBI agents thought about magazines
   c. how the FBI drew the wrong conclusion
   d. why a magazine described the bomb

_____ **4.** The story mainly tells:
   a. why some people were whipped
   b. why the Puritans hated England
   c. how the Puritans continued an injustice
   d. how the king felt about the Puritans of England

_____ **5.** The story mainly tells:
   a. what thing is used to read the product codes
   b. how the product code system works
   c. whether the machine reads the number or the bars
   d. how the numbers are assigned to companies

Unit 20

1. A Cherokee named Sequoya developed an alphabet for his people. The work took twelve years. He made 85 signs for the sounds in the language. Soon people learned the new language. Books and papers were printed in Cherokee. Cherokee people could write the history of their ancient culture and pass their knowledge to other people.

2. An insect was ruining Australian sugarcane. A toad was imported from South America to eat the bugs. The three-pound toad ate the sugarcane insects. It then ate crops, other toads, and helpful bugs. The toads poisoned the dogs, cats, and cattle that tried to eat them. The toads also multiplied quickly. Officials offered $30 for each toad—dead or alive.

3. Shock may occur after a bad accident, heart attack, or poisoning. A person in shock is pale and cold. The heartbeat and breathing are weak and fast. What can you do if someone is in shock? Call a doctor. Keep the victim warm and quiet until the doctor comes. Don't try to move the sick person. Shock can kill a person who has even minor injuries.

4. A Dutch artist once painted pictures and signed them with the names of famous artists. Some of these pictures were sold to Nazi officers. After World War II, the artist was arrested for selling art treasures to the enemy. People didn't believe the pictures he sold were fakes. He had to paint a picture in jail before they believed him.

5. Saffron comes from the crocus plant and costs about two thousand dollars a pound! Over seventy thousand crocuses must be picked by hand to get one pound of saffron. In the Middle Ages, people who grew and sold saffron became very rich. Saffron was so valuable that smuggling crocus bulbs was punishable by death!

_____ **1.** The story mainly tells:
     a. how long Sequoya worked on his alphabet
     b. how many symbols the Cherokee language has
     c. how Cherokee became a written language
     d. how many books were printed in Cherokee

_____ **2.** The story mainly tells:
     a. how big the South American toad was
     b. what happened when the toad came to Australia
     c. what kind of animals were poisoned
     d. how much the toads were worth to officials

_____ **3.** The story mainly tells:
     a. how to recognize and treat shock
     b. when shock is likely to occur
     c. what can happen to a person in shock
     d. how to treat all accident victims

_____ **4.** The story mainly tells:
     a. why the artist was arrested after the war
     b. how a greedy artist got into trouble
     c. who bought the fake pictures from the artist
     d. how the artist proved he had painted the pictures

_____ **5.** The story mainly tells:
     a. why crocus smuggling was punishable by death
     b. how expensive saffron has always been
     c. how much saffron costs today
     d. when people grew very rich

1. Native Americans dried meat and crumbled it, then mixed it with fat. Sometimes they added berries and sugar. This *pemmican* didn't spoil, and it provided lots of energy for people traveling or going to war. Today explorers still carry this food.

2. Lambs are sometimes eaten by coyotes, so ranchers may hunt or trap the coyotes to stop losses. But killing coyotes may upset nature's balance. Scientists have found a way to protect sheep without killing coyotes. Coyotes are fed lamb meat treated with a drug. When they eat the meat, they get sick. Later, coyotes won't even get near lambs. They hunt rabbits instead.

3. For years, food chemists have tasted hot peppers for chili sauce, catsup, and pizza. But people had a hard time telling how spicy the peppers were. After eating two or three, their taste buds were burning. Now a machine can test different kinds of hot peppers. It measures the chemicals in the peppers that provide the spicy taste.

4. The spots on a fawn's coat let it hide in shady areas without being seen. The Viceroy butterfly looks like the bad-tasting Monarch, so birds avoid both. The hognose snake hisses and rolls in its back when afraid. When it is attacked, the opossum plays dead. Upset turtles hide in their shells until they are sure it's safe to come out again.

5. The temperature in Antarctica once fell to 128 degrees below zero. In the summertime, temperatures average well below freezing. Most of the land is covered with ice up to two miles thick. Only a few strong mosses and sturdy spiders can live on this big block of ice. Since very little snow or rain falls there, Antarctica is called a desert.

_____ **1.** The story mainly tells:
  a. who uses pemmican today
  b. what can be put in pemmican
  c. what pemmican is
  d. why people use pemmican

_____ **2.** The story mainly tells:
  a. why coyotes prefer rabbits to lambs
  b. why killing coyotes upsets nature's balance
  c. how scientists protect sheep and coyotes
  d. what kind of people do not like coyotes

_____ **3.** The story mainly tells:
  a. how scientists measure chemicals
  b. what hot and spicy peppers are used for
  c. why people have trouble tasting hot peppers
  d. how a machine helps the hot pepper industry

_____ **4.** The story mainly tells:
  a. how some animals protect themselves
  b. why some harmless animals look like dangerous ones
  c. why spots or stripes make animals less visible
  d. why birds don't like Monarch butterflies

_____ **5.** The story mainly tells:
  a. what Antarctica is like
  b. which plants and insects live in Antarctica
  c. how much snow and rain fall there
  d. how low the temperature once fell

1.   Gold has been used as money, in jewelry, and as ornaments. Dentists use gold to fill teeth. Gold can be hammered so fine that light shines through it. Gold is used in office building windows to reduce the drain on the air conditioning.

2.   Some Americans who died in wars couldn't be identified, but people wanted to honor these brave men and women. A lovely tomb was built in Virginia. A few of these unknown soldiers were buried here. They represent all the soldiers who were never identified. The Tomb of the Unknown Soldier is guarded 24 hours a day. It is an honor to be a sentry at this monument.

3.   In 1815 Mount Tambora blew its top. The huge blast took 4,000 feet off Tambora's top and killed 12,000 people. The dust from the explosion spread around the world, blocking sunlight. Europe and America were unusually cold the next year. Ten inches of snow fell in New England in June. People called 1816 *the year without summer.*

4.   A hundred viruses placed side by side would be no wider than a human hair. But these small germs cause over 50 diseases. Chicken pox, colds, and rabies are all caused by viruses. Over 21 million people died because of "flu" caused by these germs. Scientists are trying to find new ways to get rid of these tiny killers.

5.   Stevie Wonder said, "Reading a letter puts me in a total one-to-one relationship with the person the letter is from." He thinks the telephone keeps people from communicating. On the phone, there's too much distance and all those wires between people. Wonder thinks that letters are a private form of expression. "It's all very direct and intense," he said. "The letters that move me the most are the ones that are honest."

_____ 1. The story mainly tells:
   a. why gold is used in jewelry
   b. what gold is used for
   c. how gold is hammered
   d. how office buildings have gold windows

_____ 2. The story mainly tells:
   a. why the soldiers could not be identified
   b. where the Tomb of the Unknown Soldier is
   c. why the Tomb is guarded all the time
   d. why the Tomb of the Unknown Soldier was created

_____ 3. The story mainly tells:
   a. how many people died because of Mount Tambora
   b. how the explosion of a volcano can affect weather
   c. what name people gave to the year 1816
   d. how much snow fell in New England in June

_____ 4. The story mainly tells:
   a. how small viruses cause many diseases
   b. how many people died from "flu"
   c. how chicken pox is caused
   d. how many people died because of viruses

_____ 5. The story mainly tells:
   a. how Stevie Wonder writes honest letters
   b. when letters are private
   c. how telephones help people communicate
   d. why Stevie Wonder likes letters

Score

49

1. In real life, rattlers seldom attack. The snakes try to avoid people. Most people are bitten only after they step on a snake. Also, a rattler may not inject its poison when it bites. In fact, more Americans die from insect stings than from snakebites.

2. Air plants, like mosses and lichens, grow on buildings and stones. They get their food and water from the air around them. Other plants, like mistletoe, get their food and water from the trees they live in. Sometimes the trees may die if these plants take away too much food or water.

3. Alfred Nobel invented dynamite to help builders. But it was used for war, and he hated that. He felt guilty that his invention was being misused. He was a rich man, and he set up a fund with nine million dollars. The fund is used today to reward people who have improved human life. *Nobel Prizes* are now given in six fields, including peace, medicine, and chemistry.

4. The rare Chinese panda lives on tender young bamboo shoots. But most all bamboo dies at the same time, right after flowering. Without the bamboo plant, the pandas starve. Some people fear the rare pandas may die out. In some places, food is given to the hungry animals. Some are airlifted to places where the bamboo is still alive.

5. Bob Geldof talked to the top musical talents of the world and asked them to sing at a concert to raise money. The stars said, "Yes!" So Geldof found a stadium, arranged for TV coverage, and set up a trust fund. He said that none of the stars would get special treatment. Everyone would work together. In 1985, the Live Aid concert raised over $100 million for starving children.

_____ 1. The story mainly tells:
   a. when rattlesnakes use their poison
   b. why insects kill people
   c. why rattlers aren't very dangerous
   d. how snakes bite

_____ 2. The story mainly tells:
   a. what kinds of plants grow on buildings
   b. why mistletoe sometimes kills trees
   c. how some plants don't live in soil
   d. how mosses and lichens get food and water

_____ 3. The story mainly tells:
   a. what the Nobel Prizes are given for
   b. why Nobel founded the Nobel Prize fund
   c. how much money was set aside for rewards
   d. what invention Alfred Nobel created

_____ 4. The story mainly tells:
   a. what the Chinese pandas usually eat
   b. how the bamboo plants flower
   c. how people are keeping pandas alive
   d. why pandas sometimes starve to death

_____ 5. The story mainly tells:
   a. how Bob Geldof found a stadium
   b. what the stars said when asked to sing
   c. why people are hungry in Africa
   d. how Bob Geldof worked to raise money

Unit 24

1. Kitty O'Neil, bored by housework, wanted to become a stunt person. Now she performs incredible stunts, like one hundred-foot falls. O'Neil has been deaf since she was a baby. But she says she can concentrate better than most hearing people. She is not bothered by the sounds around her.

2. Some scientists have been giving animals' brains small, painless electric shocks. Some beasts fall asleep, while others get angry or scared. An enraged bull whose brain is shocked may suddenly stop while he is charging. These tests help us find out which parts of the brain control behavior.

3. Hungry deer do millions of dollars worth of damage to young pine trees yearly. But scientists in Washington have found a way to protect the trees. They use a substance called *selenium*. Selenium produces a bad smell when dissolved. A bit of this element is put in the ground near trees. Rain dissolves the selenium and the tree absorbs it. The bad smell keeps the deer away until the tree is grown.

4. Edith Cavell saved many lives during World War I. She was in charge of a hospital in Belgium. American and British soldiers hid at her hospital. She helped about two hundred of them escape from their enemies. Later, she was shot for her brave actions. Her last words were, "Patriotism is not enough." A mountain in Canada is named in Edith Cavell's honor.

5. Sharks have a keen sense of hearing and can smell blood from almost two thousand yards away. Sharks also have a special system of channels in their skin that helps them feel the vibrations of a struggling swimmer. We know that in clear water, sharks can see dinner from about 50 feet away. So always swim away smoothly if sharks are spotted.

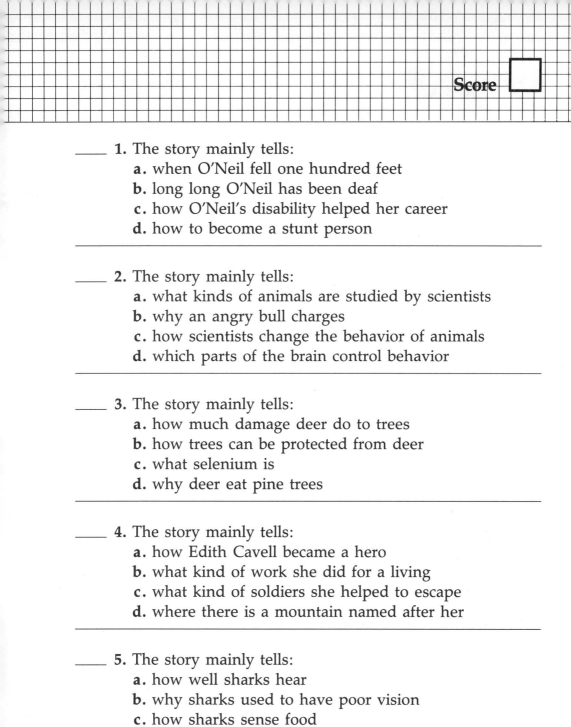

____ 1. The story mainly tells:
    a. when O'Neil fell one hundred feet
    b. long long O'Neil has been deaf
    c. how O'Neil's disability helped her career
    d. how to become a stunt person

____ 2. The story mainly tells:
    a. what kinds of animals are studied by scientists
    b. why an angry bull charges
    c. how scientists change the behavior of animals
    d. which parts of the brain control behavior

____ 3. The story mainly tells:
    a. how much damage deer do to trees
    b. how trees can be protected from deer
    c. what selenium is
    d. why deer eat pine trees

____ 4. The story mainly tells:
    a. how Edith Cavell became a hero
    b. what kind of work she did for a living
    c. what kind of soldiers she helped to escape
    d. where there is a mountain named after her

____ 5. The story mainly tells:
    a. how well sharks hear
    b. why sharks used to have poor vision
    c. how sharks sense food
    d. when to swim away smoothly

Score

53

1.   In colonial times, women were printers, whalers, and blacksmiths. Now women are fighting hard to get some of these jobs. For years, men didn't deliver babies, but now many doctors are male. A woman's work used to be sewing, cooking, and raising children. But in 1960, the first female prime minister in the world was elected.

2.   The Masai of East Africa raise cattle for a living. Very little grain is raised in the area, so the people depend on the cattle for food. Most people drink a gallon of milk a day, and beef is a popular meat. Cow's blood is also used as food. It doesn't spoil, it provides protein and minerals, and it can be taken from cows while traveling.

3.   Allied soldiers in World War II were trapped at Dunkirk, France. They couldn't escape. The shallow water kept rescue ships from landing. But hundreds of people in England took rowboats, tugs, and barges across the English Channel. For eight days, this odd navy carried soldiers from the beaches to the large ships. Over three hundred thousand soldiers were taken to safety.

4.   Plant experts in Bolivia found some odd potatoes. Their leaves make a sticky glue. Insects that walk on the plant get caught and starve. Scientists want to breed more potatoes with these sticky leaves. Farmers could grow potatoes and they wouldn't have to spray their plants with chemicals to get rid of insects.

5.   Aluminum used to be a very expensive metal. It cost over five hundred dollars a pound. But in 1886, two scientists dicovered a way to make the metal more cheaply. Two years later, another scientist refined the process even more. Then the price of the metal was less than thirty cents a pound. Now aluminum is so cheap that it is often thrown away.

_____ **1.** The story mainly tells:
  a. how men's and women's jobs have changed
  b. how women fought for work
  c. why many men are now doctors
  d. when the first prime minister was elected

_____ **2.** The story mainly tells:
  a. how much grain is raised in the world
  b. what odd foods people eat in different areas
  c. how cows provide the Masai with food
  d. what kind of cattle the Masai raise

_____ **3.** The story mainly tells:
  a. why small ships are better than big ships
  b. how many soldiers were saved
  c. how soldiers were rescued from Dunkirk
  d. why the big ships couldn't get into shallow water

_____ **4.** The story mainly tells:
  a. how insects are caught by the plants
  b. where the special potato plants grow
  c. how a special potato plant may help farmers
  d. why chemicals are used to kill bugs

_____ **5.** The story mainly tells:
  a. how much aluminum used to cost
  b. how the price of aluminum has changed
  c. how scientists refined a process
  d. what makes aluminum strong

Shaping Up

Sometimes a main idea can be seen in pictures instead of words. Look at each shape. Tell what the shape reminds you of. The first one has been done for you.

1. *table, house, bench, swing frame*	
2. _____	
3. _____	
4. _____	
5. _____	
6. _____	
7. _____	
8. _____	
9. _____	
10. _____	

Do You Get It?

What main idea is expressed by each group of words? (The first one is done for you.)

1. *love   happiness   contentment   loneliness   worry   anger*
Main idea: *different kinds of feelings*

2. *capitals   language   area   people   national song*
Main idea: _____

3. *ant   giraffe   colors   plants   shapes   dogs   turtle*
Main idea: _____

4. *thaw   warmth   seeds   buds   planting gardens*
Main idea: _____

5. *Harriet Tubman   Martin Luther King   Jackie Robinson*
Main idea: _____

6. *swan   goose   sea gull   pelican   duck   penguin*
Main idea: _____

7. *microphone   Elvis Presley   guitar   Stevie Wonder*
Main idea: _____

What's on TV?

Make up the details of a TV story after reading the main idea.

1. *Main Idea for a TV Story*

   A very shy young man works at a flower shop. He is sent by the owner to deliver some flowers and to sing "Happy Birthday" at the door of someone's house.

   Details
   Names for the young man, the owner, the birthday person:

   _____

   What happens when the young man delivers the flowers?

   _____
   _____
   _____
   _____

2. *Main Idea for a TV Story*

   A young woman does not want to lend her car to a friend who is a careless driver.

   Details
   Names for the young woman and her friend:

   _____

   What is the conversation between the young woman and her friend?

   _____
   _____
   _____
   _____

Sign Language

Signs that will be read by drivers on the road have to be short and to the point. The colors of the letters and background have to be easy to see.

Write signs for the following purposes, and give the colors you would use for words and background. You can include simple diagrams on the sign.

1. A shop ¼ mile down the road on the left sells baskets, rugs, and other arts and crafts made by the Navajo people. It is open during the day only.

Colors: _____

2. Drivers are approaching a very narrow bridge that goes over a creek. It is difficult to see this bridge at night.

Colors: _____

3. A zoo is off the road on the right about ½ mile away. People can look at the animals and have lunch in the restaurant.

Colors: _____

Check yourself

Main Idea 2

Unit *1*	Unit *2*	Unit *3*	Unit *4*	Unit *5*	Unit *6*	Unit *7*	Unit *8*
1. b	1. b	1. c	1. d	1. c	1. a	1. d	1. b
2. d	2. b	2. c	2. b	2. c	2. b	2. c	2. b
3. d	3. a	3. c	3. c	3. a	3. c	3. c	3. b
4. c	4. c	4. c	4. c	4. c	4. c	4. a	4. c
5. d	5. a	5. c	5. d	5. d	5. c	5. b	5. c

Unit 9	Unit 10	Unit 11	Unit 12	Unit 13	Unit 14	Unit 15	Unit 16
1. c	1. a	1. b	1. c	1. a	1. b	1. b	1. b
2. c	2. b	2. b	2. d	2. a	2. b	2. a	2. a
3. b	3. b	3. d	3. c	3. b	3. c	3. c	3. b
4. c	4. d	4. a	4. b	4. c	4. c	4. a	4. c
5. d	5. a	5. a	5. a	5. d	5. a	5. d	5. b

Unit *17*	Unit *18*	Unit *19*	Unit *20*	Unit *21*	Unit *22*	Unit *23*	Unit *24*	Unit *25*
1. b	1. b	1. c	1. c	1. c	1. b	1. c	1. c	1. a
2. c	2. b	2. c	2. b	2. c	2. d	2. c	2. c	2. c
3. c	3. a	3. c	3. a	3. d	3. b	3. b	3. b	3. c
4. b	4. c	4. c	4. b	4. a	4. a	4. c	4. a	4. c
5. c	5. c	5. b	5. b	5. a	5. d	5. d	5. c	5. b